GIN RUMMY
HOW TO PLAY AND WIN

Sam Fry

D1248882

DOVER PUBLICATIONS, INC.
NEW YORK

Copyright © 1960, 1978 by Sam Fry, Jr.
All rights reserved under Pan American and
International Copyright Conventions.

Published in Canada by General Publishing
Company, Ltd., 30 Lesmill Road, Don Mills,
Toronto, Ontario.
Published in the United Kingdom by Constable
and Company, Ltd., 10 Orange Street, London
WC2H 7EG.

This Dover edition, first published in 1978, is
a revised republication of the work first released
serially in 28 installments by King Features Syndi-
cate, Inc., New York, in 1960 under the title *How
to Play Gin Rummy*.

International Standard Book Number:
0-486-23630-7
Library of Congress Catalog Card Number:
77-99248

Manufactured in the United States of America
Dover Publications, Inc.
180 Varick Street
New York, N.Y. 10014

CONTENTS

1.

INTRODUCTION:
THE RULES OF THE GAME

Practically everybody plays some game in the Rummy family. Hundreds of different types of Rummy games are played throughout the country. (Canasta and Mahjongg are blood relatives of them and of each other.) But most of those hundreds of games are dying out. Why? Because Rummy players all over the country are turning, or have turned, to Gin Rummy, forsaking their old loves and concentrating on this delightful and scientific version.

The Gin Rummy buff is a real dyed-in-the-wool devotee of his favorite game. His family sees very little of him unless they play too. To him baseball is for small boys, bridge for eggheads and women, golf for out-of-door fiends, movies and television for lazy people, poker for tough guys and canasta for sissies. But Gin Rummy—that's for him!

He is a small businessman or a corporation director, an accountant or a doctor, a Hollywood producer or a Broadway musical-comedy star, a big-league ball player or a big-time golf pro. His favorite war cry is either "Gin!" or "Off the skunk!"

Gin Rummy has been popular and is gaining in popularity for a variety of reasons. Although, as we shall see, it is a game of great skill, its basic rules are simple to learn—a young child can play *at* it. Although it can be and is played by four or six or eight people together, it is essentially a two-handed contest—you don't have the problem of scurrying about looking for a "third" and a "fourth." You don't have to devote a whole evening or night to the game (although most of its devotees do); it lends itself to killing an odd half-hour or hour in a game or two.

Gin Rummy is greatly underrated as a game of skill. It is true that a good Gin Rummy player can be, and frequently is, "killed" by a near beginner over a short, one-or-two-hour session. It is also true that two good bridge players faced by two weak opponents will more frequently be able to protect themselves from such a killing in a short session. But, believe us, the good Gin Rummy player will be almost equally sure to keep well ahead on balance if he plays at all frequently.

The correct, or percentage, play does go wrong at Gin Rummy alarmingly frequently, we admit, and similarly the bad play very often works out quite well. But, by the same token, a slugging center fielder hits many a 400-foot screaming liner right into an outfielder's hands, and the weak-hitting pitcher frequently has a blooper drop in for a hit just barely over the second baseman's head. But no one ever suggests having the pitcher pinch-hit for the slugger.

Remember that up to 30 plays are made on every Gin hand (and how many hands a session do *you* play?). So it shouldn't take too long for the percentages to start asserting themselves and the skillful player to prevail.

For the benefit of those few who haven't played Gin Rummy before, and would like to, we will now give the basic rules of the game. Players with experience, fans and fanatics, may leave us now and go on to the next chapter.

THE DEAL: Taking the standard 52-card pack, 10 cards are dealt to each of the two players. The next (21st) card is dealt face up on the table. It is called the up-card. The remainder of the deck is placed alongside this card and becomes what is known as the stock (or the wall, or the pack, etc.).

THE PLAY: The non-dealer is the first player and he has the privilege of taking up the up-card dealt for his hand or refusing it. If he takes it up, he discards a card from his hand (face up on the table) in its stead. If he refuses it, the dealer has the privilege of taking it up and discarding, or of refusing it. If both refuse, then the first player takes a card from the stock and discards one from his hand, putting it face up on top of the first card turned up. The dealer then may take his opponent's discard or a card from the stock, after which he discards. So the play progresses. Each player in turn either takes up his opponent's last discard (the top card on the pile) or draws from the stock and then discards. The hand ends when either player "knocks," or "goes down" (to be explained shortly).

THE BASIC OBJECTIVE—MAKING MELDS IN YOUR HAND: A meld consists either of a minimum of three cards of the same denomination (obviously four is the maximum) or three *or more* cards of the same suit in touching sequence. The Ace is low only for sequences, the King then being high. The following are typical melds:

THE ULTIMATE OBJECTIVE: The objective of the game is to get all of one's cards matched into melds, or *enough of them so matched* that one may knock or go down. One may knock or go down (in the standard version of the game) if one's unmatched cards—those not in legal melds—add up to 10 points or less. An Ace counts one point, a 2 two points, a 3 three points, and so on through the 10. All picture cards count 10 points. Although we are going to devote quite a bit of space later on to a very popular variation of Gin Rummy called Oklahoma Gin, in which you cannot always "knock" or "go down" for 10 points, the up-card determining the number, the primary game is based on going down for anything up to and including 10. That will be our chief concern for the first few chapters. The most typical knocking and (you hope) winning hand consists of two spreads or melds and four small cards. Something like:

The hand ends when a player knocks. His opponent, with (presumably) more points in unmatched cards in his hand, loses the difference in points.

If a player knocks for zero—that is, with all of the cards in his hand used in melds—he is considered to have gone Gin. There is an extra bonus for this.

If, when one player knocks, his opponent happens to have fewer points in unmelded cards in his hand than the number that the player knocked for, this is known as an undercut. There is a special bonus for this, too.

When your opponent knocks, or goes down, you may "play off" on his melds any unmatched cards of your own which legitimately fit on them, thus reducing your point loss. (You may play a King on his three Kings; the heart 10 or 6 on his 9-8-7 heart run.)

We'll go into the scoring in the next chapter.

2.

THE STANDARD GAME

A summary of the scoring at standard, two-handed Gin Rummy is in order. We suggested, when we gave the basic rules of the game in the first chapter, that experienced players leave us for the nonce. But, what with the myriad of scoring variations—state rules, city rules, club rules, house rules—everyone had better stick around for this. Let's make sure, for future reference, that we're speaking the same language. The following is the most generally accepted scoring for Standard Gin Rummy.

Regardless of the number of the up-turned card on the deal, you may "knock" or go down with 10 points (or less) in unmatched cards. You enter on your side of the score pad the difference in points between what you knocked for and the point total of the unmatched cards in your opponent's hand.

If you go Gin—that is, go down with your entire hand melded and no unmatched cards—you get a 25-point bonus added to the points with which you caught your opponent. This entry is put in your column in one total figure (14 points plus 25 for Ginning: enter 39).

If your opponent goes down for 8 points and you have only 6 in your hand, you get the two-point difference, plus a 20-point bonus for undercutting him. This is also entered as one figure.

Each time either player scores, the points are added to his previous total. The player first reaching 100 points is the winner. He gets a 100-point game bonus plus the difference between his point total and the opponent's.

Also, 20 points are awarded for each box for each player; a box simply means a won hand, regardless of number of points scored. In other words, each entry in the scoring column is a box.

If the winner has scored 6 boxes to his opponent's 4, he gets 40 points more added to the game bonus and point-spread total. The loser may have scored more boxes than the winner; in such a case he will accordingly cut down his total point loss, at the same rate of 20 points a box differential.

If the losing player hasn't scored at all by the game's completion, the winner's total score is doubled. This is known as a "schneider" or a "skunk" or a "blitz"—depending on where you live.

Assuming *this scoring* and the *10-point knock* we come to our first major lesson point. Our primary objective is to go down as rapidly as possible with 10 points or less and win the box and as many points as the gods of chance, and our opponent, have allowed us. Despite the name of the game, going for Gin and gunning for that 25-point bonus is only a secondary or incidental objective. It's nice work, if you can get it, to be able to go down early with some such completely matched hand as:

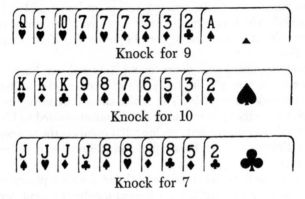

But don't go for it unless your hand is such that you are forced to such a course of action, or unless it is late in the hand and you know your opponent is down very low and waiting to undercut you. (Later on, when we look at variations of the game with higher bonuses for going Gin, we'll see how our tactics change.)

So most of the time you are going for some such array as:

3.

THE "THIRD" SPREAD

Playing the standard game, in which one can always go down with 10 points or less (or, for that matter, playing any variation when a picture card or a 10 happens to be the up-card), we should be acutely conscious of one important thing. Here it is:

If we are playing to go Gin, we of course need three normal spreads (barring those rare hands with two five-card sequences). But in the knock-for-10-no-fancy-bonus game, we rarely play for Gin. But it is good to think of our tactics as *three-spread* tactics. The reason is that while two of our spreads will of necessity be normal—a three- or four-of-a-kind or a sequence—the "third" spread is our collection, or potential collection, of two, three or four assorted small cards adding to 10 or less.

Here are a few examples of how we play for that "third spread":

1. Our opponent has just dealt the hand and the card he has turned up is the heart 3. We have been dealt this quite reasonable array of ten cards:

We should grab up that 3 promptly, even though it seemingly ties in with nothing in our hand, and discard the useless Jack of spades. Because that 3 is actually anything but useless. It ties in with the odd 4, 2 and Ace we already have, to give us four cards adding up to 10. We will thus have our "third spread" and a four-card one at that. With the three Kings ready-made, we are now prepared for a quick down if we can get one of the four cards which will hitch on to our 7-7-6 combination.

2. It is very early in the hand. We're in luck today! After drawing from the wall these are our eleven cards:

Discard one of the 9's even though it gives up a very tempting Gin play. If we throw either low card, even if one appears "safe," we might wait all day for a 9. The other two 9's may be near the bottom of the pack, or our opponent may be using them in his business. But if we throw a 9 we are in terrific position to be down on our next play. Any Ace, 2, 3 or 4 can team up with the 4 and 2 we have retained to make our "third meld." Or the 5 or 9 of diamonds to add to our run will do the trick—with the latter a likely discard of our opponent after we have thrown a 9.

3. Again it's quite early in the game—about the third draw. These are the eleven cards before us after taking a card:

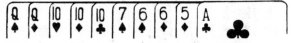

Let's assume that the spade 6 is a completely "wild" card—nothing near it has appeared on the table. Let's further assume that a 4 has been discarded and the 5 of hearts also, making our heart 4 quite a safe-appearing discard. Throw the 6 anyway. Discarding the 4 would, in effect, break up a four-card spread. By keeping our four low cards adding to 10 or less, we are retaining our quick-out position if we can just hit that 9-9-8 combination.

4. Of course a goodly number of hands call for playing for that third spread to be a real one. Suppose, at our second turn, our opponent throws a Queen. Our ten cards are:

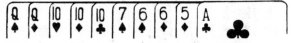

Of course we pick up the Queen, and we discard the *Ace!* We're going for a legitimate third meld here; looking for two or three more low cards to go with the Ace would surely be the "hard way." Since a third meld is our objective, we might as well go all out with it and have *all combinations* running for us. By making this play we're not particularly trying to Gin the hand. For example: If we pick up a 6 on our next play, we'll go down for five and expect a fair haul. But if the hand runs along a while, and playing for Gin seems necessary or expedient, we're in a good position to do so.

4.

OFFENSIVE COMBINATIONS

The secret of playing good Gin is trying to achieve a proper balance between offensive and defensive play. Pure offensive play consists of building up one's own hand to the nth degree, keeping all combinations and discarding useless wild cards at random. Defensive play consists of trying whenever possible to throw a card which you know your opponent cannot or probably cannot use, sometimes breaking up your hand to do so.

These safe discards are determined by an inspection (or recollection) of the previous discards plus the cards in your own hand. When you make such a safe discard you don't completely stop your opponent; he still may make a fine draw from the stock. But you've at least reduced his chances.

Several future chapters will discuss how to try to achieve the ideal balance between offensive and defensive discarding. For now let's survey offensive combinations and our chances of bettering them.

If you hold the King-Queen of a suit, this is a pretty poor combination. Only *one card*, the Jack of that suit, will help. The same thing holds true of any Ace-2 of a suit or any combination in a suit, such as Queen-10, 8-6, 5-3 and the like. But how about these combinations:

All of these combinations have two cards running for them to achieve a meld. In the first, either missing Queen; in the second, the diamond 10 or 7; in the third, the club 5 or 3.

These three-card combinations are an improvement:

There are three cards in each case which will produce a meld. The following are typical three-card combinations which offer four openings for a meld:

Here is a typical six-card combination that is a beauty. Cherish it (or its relatives) whenever you're lucky enough to get it:

Note that this combination now contains one meld, but only one meld. You can count either the three 8's or the spade sequence, but not both. But look how many cards are available to change these six cards into two melds. The fourth 8; either of two missing 7's; the heart 9 or the heart 6 and the spade 5. A total of six cards.

Beware of certain pitfalls in combinations. If you have the 8 and 6 of spades and two 7's, neither of them spades, at first glance you seem to have one one-card opening for a meld and one two-carder. But these combinations overlap—the spade 7 can be used only once—so a total of only two cards can help either of these combinations. So you had best start discarding from either the 8-6 or the 7's, depending on the rest of your hand and the previous discards.

Be on the alert for information which can minimize the value of your combinations. You have the 9-8 of diamonds; your opponent has picked up the spade 10. You can tell from your hand or previous discards that he is using the spade 10 for tens and not a sequence. He may have all four 10's, in which case your diamond run probably is completely dead at one end; even if he has only three, it's two to one that the diamond 10 is one of them. Therefore, it looks very much as though your diamond 9-8 is open only for the 7, so that's a good spot to look to for your next discard, unless you have a completely safe one in reserve.

Incidentally, even if you have no clue at all as to why your opponent took up that 10 of spades, there's still an even chance it was for 10's. So your chances of improving your 9-8 are still reduced, even though not as much.

Similarly, suppose the heart Jack has been thrown earlier in the play. You have the heart 10 and another 10 and later pick up the heart 9. If you have a convenient discard and can thus play for the heart 8 as well as either 10, keep the heart 9. But if you have to give up one of the three cards, it's two to one, offensively speaking, to throw the heart 9 rather than one of the 10's. There are two 10's running for you, but only one 8 of hearts.

5.

SAFETY IN DISCARDING

Our over-all strategy—as to whether, in any particular hand, we should discard offensively and dangerously, or defensively and as safely as possible—will be gone into in subsequent chapters. Assuming that we want to discard as safely as possible, let's discuss the relative safety of possible discards.

We'll take at random the 10 of diamonds. No 10's, and no diamonds near the 10, have shown up in the discards or exist in our hand. This 10, therefore, if discarded, can give our opponent a meld if he has any one of *six* combinations. If he has any one of these three holdings he will pick it up for three 10's:

And if he has any one of these combinations he will pick it up for a run:

So remember that a completely wild card has six chances of being used.

The next thing to remember is that a completely wild King or Queen or Ace or 2 has some slight built-in security. The King (or Ace) is open to three combinations of Kings, as illustrated above with 10's. But any given King (or Ace) can be used in only one combination for a sequence. With the King, it's the Queen-Jack. In the case of the Ace, it's the 2-3 and nothing else. So a wild King or Ace is subject to capture by a total of four combinations instead of six—a not inconsiderable difference.

The Queen (or 2) is subject to use for a sequence by two combinations as opposed to one for the King or Ace and three for any other card. A Queen fits in nicely between a King-Jack or above a Jack-10, but that's all. So wild Queens and 2's are open to a total of five combinations. That's only one less than six, but it's something to consider.

But don't let us give the impression that we are putting Aces and deuces in the same discarding category as Kings and Queens (at least not if we are playing that you can go down for 10 points —which is the game now under discussion). Discarding wild Aces and deuces not only can give melds to the enemy, but also they are often snatched up early in the hand by the enemy for his little group of three or four cards adding up to 10 or less. A deuce or Ace (or even a 3 or 4) may provide the wherewithal for a quick down by an opponent who already has two runs. So, unless you're in pretty good shape yourself, be wary of those low discards.

The other obvious reason for being careful of low discards in the early play is reducing your own hand. Throwing a picture makes you stuck for 10 points less if your opponent goes down; a discarded 2 only saves two points.

This reducing-your-own-hand policy becomes less important, as we shall see later, in variations of the game with higher Gin bonuses and with less than 10 required for knocking.

Now back to that completely wild 10 of diamonds with which we started this little story. Suppose it's not completely wild; let's say we have the 10 of spades in our hand doing full-time duty in a nice little spade run. That 10 of diamonds is still open to three possible sequence combinations but only *one* combination of 10's (instead of *three*)—specifically the heart 10 and the club 10. So it is open to a total of only four combinations, putting it in the same safety category as a loose King—and one point better than a loose Queen, which we saw was open to a five-chance capture.

Similarly, if, along with that 10 of diamonds, we had three Jacks in our hand, including the Jack of diamonds, that 10 as a discard would again be less vulnerable to capture by *two* points. It would be open to three pair-of-10 combinations, but only one sequence combination—the 9-8.

Sticking to that wild 10 of diamonds, we can see that if only the diamond Queen is accounted for, *one* combination is eliminated and five are left open. If both the diamond Queen and diamond 9 are gone, that wild 10 is open to the three combinations of 10's and that's all—no sequence is possible.

So we can see that discarding is a matter of relative safety, decided upon by a quick mental count of the open combinations for the various dangerous cards among which we must choose.

If our opponent has just discarded a King, and we have the King and Queen of spades in our hand, it is quite obvious that the spade King provides us with a 100-per-cent-safe discard—one that is open to *no* combinations. We've already learned that a completely wild card like that poor 10 of diamonds we selected at random, with no relatives in sight from either the 10 department or the diamond department, is open to *six* combinations.

Thus there is complete safety, or no combinations, at one pole, and complete danger, in the form of six combinations, at the other. Most of the time our choice of discards will fall between cards not at either pole—open to anywhere from one to five combinations. In any clearcut situation we follow the percentages. For example, we automatically discard a useless card open to only three combinations ahead of one open to four. But if the three-way danger card is part of a potential meld *of our own*, we surely then throw away the four-way danger card which is useless to us.

Obviously the one-point difference in danger level is not worth considering with offensive factors involved at the same time. This is a completely simple and elementary example of finding the proper balance between offensive and defensive play.

Let's look at a few examples of how we determine relative safety and select a discard:

1. The up-card dealt was the spade 4, refused by you and your opponent. You draw from the stock and now have these eleven cards:

The club Jack is completely wild and open to the maximum of six combinations. The diamond 10 and the diamond 8 are both open to 5 combinations; in each case one of the three possible sequences is closed by possession of the other diamond. How about the spade 7? It is open to three combinations of sevens.

Your spade 9 stops the 7-8-9 sequence. And remember your opponent passed up the spade 4. Therefore he did not have the 5 and 6 of spades; this eliminates the 7-6-5 sequence. You are open only to the 6-7-8 possibility which, added to the sevens, makes a total of four combinations.

Admittedly the diamond 2 is not open to any sequence possibility and thus to only three combinations. But this low card, with knocking for 10 permitted, may easily be valuable to you for knocking purposes later in the play. Or, more important, your opponent may pick it up for its very lowness and thus achieve an early knock himself. So the spade 7 is clearly your best discard.

2. The up-card was the spade King, refused by both players. You draw and have this eleven-card array:

The spade Ace is open to only four combinations, but we automatically eliminate that card because of its extreme lowness. We narrow things down to a choice between the diamond Queen and the club 9, both of which are open to five of the six possible combinations. We choose the 9 first because of its "advertising" possibilities. It might easily get the heart 9 for our sequence out of our opponent's hand sooner than he would ordinarily have discarded it. It is true that the diamond Queen might elicit the diamond Jack from him, but that would only give us a fourth card on an already-made meld.

3. The heart King was dealt up and refused by both players. After drawing, this is your hand:

Naturally you don't want to break up that Q-Q-J four-way offensive combination, particularly with Kings "called" for. The club Ace is open to only three combinations; the spade 3 to four (and, if it is taken for a run, our spade 6 will become a player); and the diamond 4 is open to five combinations. But we must keep all of them because of their size—their lowness is important both offensively and defensively. So here is a case where we must discard one of our completely wild, six-combination cards, the

heart 9 or spade 6. With no clues at this early stage to our opponent's pattern of discarding, we select the heart 9 solely because
we thereby unload three more points.

Here is a relatively little-known point on safety in discarding,
but one which is very important:

The up-card happens to be an Ace, taken by our opponent,
who then throws the heart 10. After drawing from the stock our
hand is:

| K ♦ | J ♥ | 10 ♠ | 9 ♣ | 5 ♠ | 5 ♣ | 4 ♣ | 4 ♦ | 3 ♦ | 2 ♦ | A ♦ | ▲ |

Obviously none of our matched low cards is expendable at this
point; we must look for the safest discard from among those four
high cards at the left. We know the King is open to four combinations; the heart Jack rates the same, since the discarded heart
10 closes all but one sequence. Also, since the heart 10 was
thrown, our spade 10 surely won't be used for tens; hence it's
open only to three combinations, all sequences.

What about the club 9? At first glance, without cerebration, it
seems completely wild and open to all six combinations. But it is
affected, and greatly so, by the fact that our opponent has thrown
the heart 10—*even more than were our heart Jack and spade 10.*
To see why this is so, we must make one basic assumption; that
is, that on his very first discard our opponent is not likely to
have broken up any combinations. Very occasionally one's hand
is such that a pair may be split right away, but that happens too
seldom to enter into our calculations or strategy.

So how is our 9 of clubs now affected by the heart 10 discard?
First we can assume that our opponent doesn't have the club 10.
Hence our club 9 is open to only one sequence, the 8-7. Second,
based on the 10 discard, we can assume that the enemy doesn't
have the heart 9 in his hand. He might have specifically the spade
and diamond 9's, but that is the only 9 combination that is open.
So we see that our apparently wild 9 is open to a total of only
two combinations—as opposed to four, four and three respectively
for our other available discards. So we should unhesitatingly let
go of the club 9.

But beware of placing too much stock in this type of inference
in the later play. Starting with as early as your opponent's second
discard, the above-explained reasoning loses *some* of its validity,

and it loses more and more as the hand progresses. As a matter of fact, if, in the middle or late stages of a fighting hand, your opponent suddenly throws what seems like a completely wild card, you can make almost the opposite type of inference. If he throws, for example, the diamond 6, and nothing near that card has appeared in previous discards, you can bet that he has another 6 in his hand (either loose or used in a run or potential run) and very likely one or two diamonds touching, or within striking distance of, the 6.

The reader may want to know why we quibble about relative safety of discards, and worry so much about a four-point danger card as opposed to a three-pointer, and so on. "One or the other has to go on your next play anyway." This oft-uttered statement is completely fallacious. Gin Rummy is, to a great extent, a game of sparring for time. Between every two discards you make three things happen. Your opponent either takes or doesn't take your discard, he makes a discard of his own, and you draw another card.

The deductions you may be able to make from this series of events can change your planned campaign completely. The next-in-line relatively safe discard may suddenly have turned into a sure or probable player on an opponent's meld. And the wildest card in your hand may have become transformed into a completely safe or relatively safe card by your opponent's next discard.

Therefore each play you make must, barring questions of over-all strategy, be an entity in itself. The picture can change so rapidly in Gin Rummy with the three occurrences between your discards that, by the time your next discard comes, you can easily be in a brand new ball game. So all you can do at each turn is to play the percentages to the hilt. Unfortunately, your percentage play too frequently does go wrong and your "pigeon" opponent in turn gets away with an inferior discard. But that is all the more reason why you should have that little edge going for you on *every* play, if you want to be a winner in the long run. Those little differences between three- and four-point peril add up.

6.

OFFENSE VS. DEFENSE

Earlier chapters have given some hints as to how we should endeavor to find the proper balance between offense and defense. If we seem to have been emphasizing defensive play and safety in discarding, it is because winning strategy—*playing a 10-point knock*—must, in most hands, be based on a defensive, sparring-for-time approach. Later on—when we discuss variations in which we can't go down for more than, say, 3 points, or we must go Gin, and there are larger bonuses for Gin—we will see the pendulum swing the other way. Many hands will call for an all-out offense, with safety in discarding not exactly ignored, but almost so.

The main thing, with a 10-point knock and a 100-point game, is that the battle concerns points rather than boxes and Gin and undercut bonuses. We can't afford to be stuck for too many points on any one hand, if we can possibly avoid it. With a bad hand, we must endeavor to gain time, to get our hand down, so that we don't lose too much by the time our opponent knocks. We do this by exercising care in choosing safe discards, even if we have to break combinations to do so. And the word "reducer" should be very much in our lexicon.

Don't worry if you're sneered at—and called a sissy—if you see fit to take up a low card just to throw a high one. Or if, on some pretty hopeless hand, you hoard *all* your low cards just to get your count down. When you adopt the latter tactic you have a built-in second advantage. The low card you don't throw may be all your opponent needs in order to go down.

Suppose, after your first draw from the stock, you hold these cards:

| K♠ | K♥ | Q♦ | J♣ | 9♠ | 8♥ | 6♠ | 6♣ | 4♥ | 2♠ | A♣ |

Your unhappiness at seeing this horrible collection is compounded by the fact that your opponent has already grabbed the up-card, the diamond 5, presumably for a meld. (His discard, the spade 10, didn't help things any.) You are already gasping for air. But you decide to make one final bold gesture. You throw the diamond Queen—not a 6-combination wild card, but, almost as bad, a fiver. It gets by your opponent, who draws from the stock and discards the heart Queen. You draw the heart 5 from the stock which gives you—just another headache.

Tempt the fates no longer! Even though the Kings are one of your only two combinations, break them. Throw the heart King. It can't be used for a run. If your opponent has the one danger-ous combination—the two remaining Kings (which is very unlike-ly)—you will then have the other King to play on him when he goes down, saving 10 points.

The King gets by, that ogre across the table draws from the stock and ominously discards a 2, right in your face. With the spade King now 100 per cent safe (the 10 was thrown—further-more he obviously doesn't have the spade Queen), you should take that 2 and throw the King. The 2 only pairs you, but it also gets your hand down eight points. If you drew from the stock the only better card you could have picked is a 6. (You're not looking for new high-card combinations on this hand—you just want to cut down expenses.) By the time your next discard comes along, the card your opponent throws probably will have opened up another safe high discard for you.

How does this hand finally come out? You tell us—thank good-ness it was yours, not ours. Seriously, though, remember it was a very bad hand that called for drastic treatment on the defensive side.

At the other pole, suppose you pick up this lovely collection:

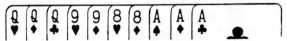

The spade 5 is the up-card, taken by your opponent. You draw the spade 6. Throw it, even though it's about even money the enemy will add it to a spade run. This is too good a hand not to go all out with. Why try to guess which one of that beautiful four-card combination of 9's and 8's to discard? If you keep all four, any one of eight cards will give you your third run. Whether you go down when you get it, or play for Gin, can be decided at the time—depending on how soon it came in, what your opponent has been doing in the meantime, how safe your discard looks, and so on.

7.

THE CAMPAIGN

If you discard a wild card on your very first play, even though it's open to the maximum of six combinations, the chances are roughly more than 3 to 1 that it won't give your opponent a meld. But if you throw an equally wild card somewhere in the middle of a hand—say at about your seventh play—the odds do a complete turnabout. In other words, at that point it's about 3 to 1 or better that your opponent *can* use the card—either for a new meld or at best (from your angle) as an addition to an existing meld in his hand.

This leads us to a principle which should have become fairly evident to any reasonably experienced player. It's simply this: The later you get in the hand, the wilder your wild cards become. Equally certain is the fact that your opponent will be more ready to knock. On *most* hands you start off—for a play or two, anyway —on the offensive, throwing cards you can't use and keeping your combinations.

The longer the hand lasts, the more careful you must become. As the stock pile grows shorter, you begin to know more and more about your opponent's hand. Suppose you suddenly draw a brand new card of a denomination (or suit) that hasn't appeared previously. If you don't *know* your opponent has two or more of that card's close relatives, you'd better assume he has. Keep that card, even at the expense of breaking up one of your offensive possibilities to find a safe discard. Otherwise he's likely to take it up and murmur in dulcet tones, "Gin, my dear friends."

Our quest for safe discards, however, sometimes gets simpler as the hand progresses. We get clues not only from what our opponent has discarded, but also from what he has taken up. And we are always helped by each new card from the stock pile which we add to our own hand.

Take these eleven cards we have to discard from, along about our sixth play on a hand:

| Q♦ | 8♠ | 7♠ | 7♥ | 7♦ | 5♣ | 4♣ | 3♣ | 4♥ | 2♥ | A♣ |

The earlier history of this deal must surely give us clues. The original up-card was the spade 3—refused by both players. Our opponent's first discard was the spade Jack. We followed it up with the spade 9 (we didn't have the 8 then), which he took for reasons then unknown to us. But by now we are 100 per cent certain that he's using the spade 9 for nines. Previous discards have been in the 6 and 5 area, plus a 7 which we took up. Except for another black Jack, no high cards have appeared.

Thus that Queen of diamonds is almost certain to hit some high-card combination our opponent is holding—either for Queens or a run. The 8 of spades, although dangerous too, is not quite as bad. We now know it can only give our opponent 8's. His three 9's stop the spade run possibility going up; our 7's stop the spade run possibility going down.

So we throw the spade 8. The heart 4 was another possibility. With the heart 6 gone and the other touching cards in our hand, it was the safest card. But we just couldn't bring ourselves to abandon all offensive possibilities.

Our spade 8 happens to get by our opponent. After drawing from the stock, he retaliates with another 8, which we pass up. We now draw the heart 5 from the stock and again have discard problems. Now that the 8's have gotten by, that diamond Queen is hotter than ever. We are tempted to keep the heart 5—since a miracle draw of the heart 3 would then Gin us—but we just can't afford it. It has to go—the Queen can hurt too much. The same thing goes for the club Ace. The latter not only can give the opponent Aces, but also can get him down low enough to knock right then and there; and anything he knocks for will be good—even if our Queen plays off. So the heart 5 goes and we now pray that our opponent's next discard or our next draw will clarify the atmosphere and get us out of the mess.

To give this story a happy ending: The 100-per-cent-safe heart 5 of course gets by and our opponent draws and throws another 8. We luckily draw an Ace and release the diamond Queen, *but only after first going down for 8 points.* Our opponent is stuck with a Q-Q-10 combination—he had hoped to get the diamond Jack if not a Queen—and we win 20-odd points plus the box.

8.

LOW CARDS

Playing with ten (or less) as the "knock" number, we have seen the importance of small cards—even completely unconnected ones—and the value of that "third meld," consisting of a package of three or more cards adding to no more than 10 points. We know this—but often we are hit below the belt emotionally by a clever opponent who teases us about playing scared in taking up those small cards just to reduce. We are mortally afraid, says he, of being stuck with a lot of points in our hand. Such an opponent is probably a pretty good Gin player, we assure you, and one with flexible scruples to boot. (In lieu of "flexible scruples" we might use one of Mr. Stephen Potter's British euphemisms and say he's adept at gamesmanship or one-upmanship.)

Knowing the value of small cards, and acting accordingly, is not sissy-like or "scared cards" or even overly defensive play. It is sound Gin Rummy tactics, and also has offensive value. All of which leads us to a firm generality (even though we feel the only true generality is that there should be no generalities). This is it: If an Ace is dealt as the up-card and you are the first player, it is compulsory to take it, almost literally, regardless of your hand. (If you are dealt a hand which is completely Gin without the Ace, the rules do not permit you to pick the Ace and *then discard it*, keeping your Gin hand intact to go down with. In such a case you have to grit your teeth and control yourself for a few seconds and let your opponent take the Ace and reduce his hand a bit. Then, after drawing from the stock, you may legally and proudly produce your Gin hand.)

Normally you must take this dealt Ace—no matter what your hand—for two reasons. One, barring very, very exceptional hands —we won't bore you with an example—you need this card, not only as a pure reducer or point-saver, but also as an offensive card. An Ace, obviously, is the best start towards that "third meld" of three or four cards adding to 10 or less. Even if you have no other low cards in your hand, it still is quite a beginning.

Equally important in taking up the Ace is keeping it from your opponent. He may even need it for a reducer for an immediate down. In any event, he can use it in almost all hands for his own potential—if not actual—"third meld" of three or more cards adding up to 10. Furthermore, if you pass it up, he can grab this Ace as a more or less "free" play. He takes it at no cost of a turn. If he didn't do so, it would just stay there, leaving you with the first move.

At the risk of over-simplification I'll go ahead and say that a 2-spot belongs in almost the same category as an Ace and for the same reasons. True, a 2 is twice as big as an Ace. (Note that a 2, without an Ace in your hand, gives only one possibility of four cards adding to 10: 3-3-2-2.) But a 2 will do until the real thing comes along.

For instance, a 2 will become part of a 2-1-2-5, or 2-1-1-6, or 2-3-5 or 2-4-4 and still add up to just the magic number. So a 2 is almost—not quite—as automatic a first-play pick as an Ace. As second player, with the dealer refusing the 2—signifying quite probably a fine hand—you may well be wary. But, in general, you take it. Remember that you do have the "free play" theory going for you. Of course your entire hand guides you in your decision. Do you have a good discard ready? What are your already-made melds and combinations and what are your small-card "third meld" possibilities?

With a 3 turned up, the first player should take it only if it gives him (a) four cards adding to 10 or less, (b) a four-way combination like 3-3-4 or a three-wayer like 3-3-5, or some cross between (a) and (b). With:

K	K	K	J	J	9	5	3	2	A	
♠	♦	♣	♥	♦	♦	♣	♥	♦	♠	▲

Surely take the club 3 as the up-card. It gives you a pair of 3's and the club 5 looms as a discard containing a modicum of safety. More important, that 3, to replace the 5, gives you four cards under 10. After taking it, any one of the three cards which hit your J-J-9 combination will give you an immediate down. Also, if the hand goes a long while, with both players then likely going for Gin, those two 3's, plus any other 3 subsequently added to your hand—may mean real pay dirt to you.

9.

TWO POINTS
OF CONTENTION

There are two points in Gin Rummy rules on which opinion is about evenly divided throughout the country. Since the official rules make both situations optional, one has no choice but to follow a "when-in-Rome" policy and do whatever the group you are with has chosen to do. I have a definite preference in both situations, and am not even sure mine is in the majority—country-wise—in either case. Naturally I, too, have to follow my playmates' wishes wherever I am.

LOOKING THROUGH THE DISCARDS

The first is this matter of whether or not you are allowed to look at the cards in the discard pile other than the last one.

Paradoxical as it may seem, most of the poorer or average players shrink in horror at such "amateurishness" and "simplification" of an already "easy" game.

On the other hand, most of the really experienced Gin Rummy sharks, including all the name bridge experts (most of whom play top-flight or nearly top-flight Gin Rummy) believe strongly that being permitted to look back improves and speeds up the game. They contend that the game requires a great deal more skill than a contest of sheer memory; they further believe (or know) that just about every *good* card player can, with a slight bit of training, learn how to memorize every discard and even the exact order in which those discards were made.

But this act of memorizing would slow up the play considerably—even the best of them would occasionally have to do a bit of mental reconstruction. Also, it would make the game more a test of routine mental labor than one of skill and imagination. Looking back makes the game more lighthearted and pleasurable and permits relinquishing concentration a bit in favor of an exchange of banter now and then. The experts who feel as I do are perfectly willing to give up some part of their "edge" over the weaker player in permitting this looking back.

The custom of "looking-backers" is to discard loosely into the center of the table. Any player who wants to check back on an earlier discard may push about the pile of loosely spread cards, and this casual research takes only a second or two. This, as opposed to the much longer (and more annoying) delays of the hard-working memorizer who must delve back into the corners of his brain to remember an early discard.

If you *do* play *no* looking back, I suggest you use one of those racks such as they have in Canasta for the discard pile, so that no one can possibly see any discard but the last one. Without a rack the discard pile must, to some extent at least, be loosely stacked and you are giving an advantage to the fellow with the keenest eyesight or the one who has become most adept at identifying a card just from seeing an exposed corner or fraction thereof.

PLAYING OFF ON GIN

The other moot point is the matter of whether or not you should be permitted to play off cards on the melds of an opponent who has Ginned you. The chief argument of those who prefer that this not be permitted is that the reward for Gin should be increased (as it would be on many hands), thus increasing the incentive to play for Gin and getting more variety in the game.

This argument is rather valid in the knock-for-10 game, but does not hold good in variations in which extra boxes or other bonuses are given for Ginning. There the incentive already exists.

My personal feeling is: Why penalize so severely the fellow who, being dealt a bad hand, has put up a heroic defensive battle? He properly keeps cards he knows to be players, in a gallant effort to make the hand go to the wall; he masterfully keeps other cards which he doesn't know for sure his opponent can use, but mathematically and correctly infers will help the enemy. Why should this stalwart defender, when his opponent luckily picks his one remaining Gin card from the wall, have to pay not only the box, the extra 25 points, the extra bonuses (if such is the game), but also all the points for the players he has held up?

The answer offered to that is that you can adapt yourself to the rules you are playing, and not hold up all those cards which are or may be players in a desperate effort to fend off what may be the inevitable; take your licking quickly and like a man. I agree that you can, to a large extent, adapt your game. So, whichever way the group likes to do it, don't make an issue of it. Go along with them.

But we firmly believe that giving bigger Gin bonuses, but permitting laying off, makes a better game.

10.

"ROUND THE CORNER"

This seems as good a time as any to introduce—and possibly dismiss for better or worse—a variation of Gin Rummy which has obtained a definite vogue here and there through the country. It's called "Round the Corner." It doesn't do the basic game any harm, but poses new problems and suggests different techniques for the true aficionado.

For simplicity's sake, let's assume the base scoring and format we have been discussing to date. One game is being played at a time (see "Hollywood Gin" in the next chapter), there's a 25-point bonus for Gin, and 10 or less is the permanent knock card. The basic difference in this variation is that we can meld "around the corner" for sequences. Aces and Kings lose their previous proud positions as stop points and become just other numbers, in an endless cycle. Any sequence may run. Starting arbitrarily at, say, 5, we run along: 5, 6, 7, 8, 9, 10, J, Q, K, A, 2, 3, 4, 5, 6—and so on *ad infinitum.* Thus, in addition to normal runs in the regular game—such as 8-9-10-J, 5-6-7, K-Q-J and A-2-3—the following also are legitimate melds:

The other major rules change, if your pals like to play "Round the Corner," is that an Ace, instead of being almost a free-ride card if your opponent knocks and you're stuck with it, becomes instead a real hot potato. Instead of counting only one measly point for your victorious opponent when you hold it, mateless, in your losing hand, it counts 15—count 'em, 15—points against you. (And in some games it is scored as 25 points when caught in your hand. But this is an even more esoteric version.) Also—and this is very important—it counts as 15 points, not one, for going-down purposes; thus making it less than useless in this direction.

If you're trapped in a "Round the Corner" game, there are three almost equally important things you have to remember, if you want to play the game well and not be a prime pigeon:

First, a K-Q or an A-K or an A-2 in the same suit has just as good a chance of being "hit" for sequence as a J-10 or 8-7 or 4-3 does in the regular game. In brief, all of these sequences are open at both ends, and with either one of two cards they become "made." Similarly, a K-2 (open to the A) or A-Q (open to the K) gives you the same one-chance possibility for a run that a 10-8 or 7-5 or K-Q or A-2 does in the normal game.

Second—and this is almost too obvious—the Ace becomes a prime candidate for early discarding just because of its sheer weight in points in case your opponent catches you by going down very early. A wild Ace, furthermore, is no longer a slightly safer discard as a meld-giver (in this game it's open to runs at *both* ends). And that difference between one point and 15 (or 25) points, if you're caught with it, is tremendous. Similarly, when it comes to splitting pairs for a discard, as an offensive-defensive maneuver, the Ace department, at 15 points a throw, takes obvious precedence over a pair of picture-card 10-pointers.

Third—and remember we're playing Round the Corner and also still playing knocking for 10 points or less—note that our so-called "third meld" becomes an objective much more difficult to attain. The Ace no longer is a candidate for part of it. The only four-card "third meld" has to be specifically 3-3-2-2. With aces out, we are also considerably restricted for a three-card "third meld." That 5-4-Ace doesn't work for us; nor does the 5-3-Ace, 7-2-Ace, or 3-2-Ace. But don't forget that three-card groups such as 4-4-2 or 3-5-2 or 4-3-2 or 3-3-4 or 2-2-3 are still working for us.

Thus, though we must fully realize that the "two three-card melds plus four small cards" hand is no longer a very likely quick-knock possibility, we still don't have to go *all out* for three runs or going Gin. True, there exists a strong and legitimate temptation to go for Gin a bit more often, but, without extra Gin bonuses (not at present under discussion), the quick knock should still be the prime objective in "Round the Corner." So be very much aware that a hand with two runs, one a *four-carder*, combined with only *three cards* adding to 10 points or less, is a *very* attainable early objective.

11.

HOLLYWOOD GIN

Most Gin Players today like to play three games at a time and the name Hollywood Gin means just that and nothing more. You can play three games at a time in the standard knock-for-10 games; you can do it in Round the Corner; and you can do it in the knock-for-the-up-card version still to be discussed.

We assume three games at a time was called Hollywood because it started there. And it's logical to us that it started there, because where else would they want to dream up a way to almost triple the stakes, but mildly camouflage the fact that they are doing so. For that's just about what you do when you play three games at a time. But the game also lends itself to some variations in playing technique, and provides the added excitement of unusual situations.

For the benefit of the uninitiated, we will explain briefly the Hollywood scoring method. You don't start off slap-bang on the first hand with the winner getting his points in his column on all three scorepads. If you did that, nothing at all would be added to the regular game. That would be the same as one game at three times the stake. Instead, each player has to earn his way to getting on all three scores, one game at a time.

Let's say I'm playing you and you win 19 points on the first hand we play. Here's how the three scores will look at this point:

ME	YOU	ME	YOU	ME	YOU
	19				

Let's say you then win 56 points, including Gin, from me on the second deal and 21 more points on the third deal. Here's how the three scores will look:

ME	YOU	ME	YOU	ME	YOU
	19		56		21
	75		75		
	96				

You of course will now get your score in all three games if you win the next hand and will continue doing so until any game or games are over. But I manage to win 15 points on the next hand. I am entitled to enter that in the first game only. Then you win 27 points on the fifth hand and here's how the score looks at this point:

ME	YOU	ME	YOU	ME	YOU
15	19		56		21
	75		75		48
	96		102		
	123				

It's obvious that the first two games are over and you've skunked me in the second game to boot. (I'll let you, the winner, figure out how many points you've won on them.) Then on the next hand I win 42 points. It goes on game three only, since the other two are finished. Here's a last look at the score, games one and two being unchanged:

ME	YOU	ME	YOU	ME	YOU
15	19		56	42	21
	75		75		48
	96		102		
	123				

Play continues on game three only, until one of us gets up to 100.

It should be easy to see that the important thing in Hollywood is to "get on" all three scores as expeditiously as possible. And not only to avoid "skunks." If you win the first hand, you are in a position to get twice as much if you win the second as your opponent will get if he wins it. And if you win the first two hands you will get three times as much for winning the third as your opponent will if he wins it.

So, on the early hands, you must go all out to get on the score and let the striving for Gin bonuses come later, if at all. Say it's the very first deal. Suppose, after drawing at about your seventh play, these are your eleven cards:

Normally, you might play this hand for Gin, throwing the heart 6. It's relatively late in the play and you don't expect to catch your opponent for many points. Your Gin chances (five cards) are excellent and the heart 6 is a pretty safe-looking discard. But at Hollywood you should knock immediately for three. Be content with a small profit, since it also includes *getting on that first game.* Otherwise your opponent might get lucky, improve his hand rapidly and Gin you instead. Then you'll be behind the eight-ball for hand two, instead of him.

12.

OKLAHOMA GIN

Up to now our discussions of technique of play have referred to the standard knock-for-10 game. In the past few years a variation of the game called Oklahoma Gin has had a terrific, still-continuing and, we think, well-deserved vogue. In the big cities it is played far more frequently than the standard game. We're sure it's here to stay.

Although there are minor variations in the rules and scoring at individual clubs, or between one community and another, Oklahoma Gin differs basically from the standard game as follows:

The dealt up-card determines the most points you may knock for. If it's a 10 or any picture card you may knock for 10 as in the standard game. If it's an 8 you can't knock for more than 8 points; if it's a 6 you need to be down to 6 points or less; if it's a 2 you can knock for 2 points, 1 point, or go Gin. If the up-card is an Ace, the rule is that you must go for Gin; knocking for 1 point in that case is not permitted. Suffice it to state that under such varying circumstances one's approach and playing technique must vary considerably, depending on the size of that up-card.

The second difference is the mystic and potent value put on the spade suit—as in pinochle and some other card games. "Spades double" is an old-time war cry to card players all over. In Gin Rummy (the Oklahoma variety) it simply means that if the up-card happens to be a spade everything counts twice as much for that deal. The number of the up-card tells you what you have to go down for; the suit of the up-card is meaningless unless it's spades. But in that case the point difference between the knocker and the knockee is doubled; any Gin or undercut bonuses added thereto are also doubled and any extra Gin or undercut boxes (still to be heard about) also are doubled.

The third difference is the "extra box" feature. The bonus for going Gin, in addition to the normal 25 points added to your point score, is *two* extra boxes. Said extra boxes are recorded on the score pad in any convenient way your group agrees upon. In any event, they count the same in the final sum-up—20 or 25 points—as normal boxes. And their value carries along only as a side account; they don't accelerate the completion of the game, which is determined by point score alone.

The undercut, being among other things a by-product of going boldly after Gin, also receives an extra bonus. To wit: one extra box in addition to the 25 points added to the point difference.

If the hand happens to be a spade hand, the extra boxes are doubled too: two instead of one for an undercut; four fat ones instead of two for Gin. All we can tell you today is that there's no known cure for a quick Gin in spades by a vicious opponent.

The fourth difference in Oklahoma Gin is that a game doesn't reach its conclusion until 150 points are attained by the leader. This is a logical rule and it's the one conservative feature in a wild, hybrid (but delicious!) version of the game. Spades, which figure to come up one time in four, double the point score; also, a low up-card forces us to play for Gin more often. Thus the Gin bonus is added to the point score more frequently. As a result, the normal 100-point game total is reached too soon. Actually 150 points can be—and frequently is—knocked off in one hand. Obviously, reaching 100 points is even more commonplace. Hence some measure of control over too-quick "skunks" is maintained by the 150-point game.

But lest you think the concocters of Oklahoma Gin went too conservative, let us add that, as a corollary to the 150-point objective, they made the game bonus 150 points instead of 100. And double for skunks remains.

Let's attempt to orient ourselves to the very different climate of Oklahoma Gin as opposed to the standard game. In getting our perspective we must keep in mind the two main differences—the size of the up- or knock-card and the increased Gin bonuses regardless of the up-card. (When a spade comes up, doubling everything, our tactics don't appreciably change, barring some state-of-the-score situation. We just need more intestinal fortitude.)

First let's inspect that up-card. If it's a 10 or picture card, we are permitted to knock with 10 points or less in unmelded cards and, in general, our plan of campaign is mapped out along those lines. Two three-card melds and four small cards, or a four- and a three-card meld with three low cards, will do the trick. A quick knock on some such modest basis mightn't open the door to great riches, but at worst it means "mission accomplished." With a 10-point knock the increased Gin bonuses affect us only slightly. And certainly when we are playing Hollywood (three games at a time), getting on the score quickly and off all three skunks is of paramount importance.

With 9 or 8 as the knock-card, our approach should vary very little, although some definite changes begin to appear. Although it begins to get a little bit more difficult to get three or four cards small enough to add to under 9 or 8, it's still not too rough. Let's take a sample opening situation:

The up-card is the heart 8 taken by our opponent, who discards the diamond 2 in exchange. An inauspicious—even ominous-appearing—beginning for us, and these are our cards:

K♠ K♦ Q♦ J♦ 9♥ 9♣ 5♠ 4♠ A♦ A♣ ●

When our opponent throws the deuce so early, with an 8-point knock, it looks as though he's got the type of hand to try for Gin, or at least a quick knock with three melds. We must try to forestall him by a counterattack with the weapons available to us. Take up the deuce—it gives us four adding up to 8, the magic number for this hand. If we can find a 9 quickly, we'll have outmarauded the marauder. The spade King gives us a safe discard, or, at any rate, one that will have to do till the real thing comes along. If, instead of getting a 9, we hit our low spade sequence on an early draw (or pick an Ace or another deuce), we'll probably then split our 9's. But even though our exact future action cannot be predicted, our immediate move is clearcut.

Let's change our hand a bit. It's the same heart 8 knock-card, taken by our opponent. The diamond 2 was discarded. Here are our cards:

K♠ K♦ Q♦ J♦ 10♣ 9♣ 9♥ 5♠ 4♠ A♦ ▲

This time we don't want that deuce, even with the spade King available for a discard. Even with the deuce in our hand we'd still need specifically another Ace to have four cards adding to 8. We're going to fight fire with fire this time, and play for three runs. We have the hand to tempt us to do it. Those potential "extra boxes," if we can Gin, will look fine in our column. Our chance for a quick knock, for defensive reasons, dovetails in this case with our chance for a big score of our own.

Suppose we draw, say, a wild 7. We throw the King. Next turn we get the spade 3 for our second run. We now should throw the diamond Ace rather than the wild 7 or part of our juicy 10-9-9 combination. The diamond Ace is safer than the 7—it can be used only for Aces; its very lowness, even with an 8 as the up-card, shouldn't disturb us. Our opponent has already thrown a deuce.

Now we are out to hit that 10-9-9 combo for our third run. When and if we hit it, we might knock for 7—or whatever our loose card is then—or play for Gin with four or five cards open to us. That will depend on how soon we hit it, and what our opponent has picked up or discarded in the meantime.

When the up-card is a 7, 6, 5 or 4, we are in what might be called the twilight zone. Playing for three melds to get down is by no means a must, but getting unmatched low cards adding up to little enough to knock gets increasingly difficult. The temptation to go for three runs is great; Gin, with extra boxes, is not to be sneered at. (Obviously Gin ensues as a very frequent by-product of playing for three runs, even though it was not at first our prime objective.) But in playing for three melds our maneuverability is limited; in trying to get those three runs, we're using up too many cards offensively, with virtually no choice of discards remaining. Thus defense is cast to the winds and our opponent may easily get the quick knock or early Gin instead of us.

To avoid overdoing playing for three melds with twilight zone up-cards (7-6-5-4), we should fix in our minds the low-card combinations that are running for us so that we can quickly recognize and use them. If 7 is the up-card, and we happen to have 3-2-A-A or 2-2-A-A, we can knock with only two three-card melds. With 6 as the up-card, only 2-2-A-A is going for us. But if we have this holding our chances for a quick down are tremendously improved.

With 5 as the knock-card, no four low-card combinations are available. But a four-card meld and a three-card meld can tie in beautifully with 2-2-A, 3-A-A, or 2-A-A. With 4 as the knock-card, only that 2-A-A is available to us. (With 6 or 7 as the up-card, 7 melded cards, of course, can tie in with many more three-low-card combinations.

But quite often we get two four-card melds or perhaps a five-card sequence and a three-carder. Suppose we've made up something like:

| Q♠ | Q♥ | Q♦ | Q♣ |　| 7♥ | 6♥ | 5♥ | 4♥ |　♥ |

It's easy to note the many two-unmatched-card combinations that will add up to (or under) seven, six, five and four respectively.

With 7 or 6 as the knock-card, we'll probably be going for three melds (and maybe Gin) slightly less than half the time; with 5 or 4, it'll average better than half the time. When we go for the two-meld, no-Gin way, it can still be an offensive maneuver, even though we give up the possibility of the fat Gin bonuses. When our hand has the requisite unmatched-low-card combination and we utilize it to go down quickly, we can often catch our opponent (who is trying earnestly to convert three fat high-card combinations into melds) with a lot of points.

But more often, particularly when we can't get down very early, the two-melds-plus-low-card knock (at 7, 6, 5 and 4) is a staving-off defensive maneuver. Suppose we start off with a bad hand. But some number of picks later (it may seem to us like a hundred) and after our opponent has taken up a couple of our discards, we may suddenly find ourselves, at a 7-knock, with something like:

| K♠ | K♥ | K♦ |　| Q♠ | Q♦ | Q♣ |　| 3♥ | 2♠ | A♦ |　| A♣ |　♟ |

We worked hard for this and it's the best we could hope for. We knock for 7, even though it's late in the day, to try valiantly to stave off the Gin that we know, or sense, our opponent is very close to. Surprisingly often we get the whole pot—our opponent was waiting with a four-card meld, a three-carder and a three-card four-way-opening combination crying to be filled. We've staved off Gin, and we've won a few points and a box on the hand. If, on the other hand, he was waiting with three made-up melds plus a low card or a player for one of our melds, we are undercut. But even then we've saved expenses a bit. His Ginning us was probably inevitable; by having to settle for an undercut, he gets one less box on each game that is going.

When the up-card is a 3, 2 or Ace, we are pretty well committed to a definite course of action. Three melds are virtually a must.

The exceptions take care of themselves—you don't go for them, you run into them. Occasionally you find you have two four-card melds and an Ace-2 (3 is the knock-card) or two four-carders and Ace-Ace (2 is the knock-card). If it's not too late in the hand you go down, and likely as not pick up quite a few points. You don't have a good Gin play anyway.

Ginning is a natural by-product of the three-meld approach. With an Ace up you must go for Gin; with a 2 or a 3 as the knock-card, you find yourself going for Gin much better than half the time. At the beginning, the extra boxes for Gin tempt you to go out for it; later, circumstances put you in a position where the effort is not likely to be costly and often is a necessity.

Remember that time is working for both players. With the low knock-card, both must be working to accumulate three melds and on most hands that takes quite a few draws. So you needn't worry too much about getting your point total down quickly, at the expense of breaking up potential melds; your opponent is having his problems, too. As far as safe discarding is concerned, the necessity for getting three melds limits your discard choices. But this is partly counteracted by the increased safety of low-card discards. They often gain safety by being related to the Ace, 2 or 3 up-card. And they lose danger because your opponent cannot take them up simply as reducers for an early knock, as he could with 10 as the up-card.

This last is an important point to remember if you are to play successfully at low knocks. Low cards not only are safer discards, but also they leave your high-card combinations intact. The fact that you may be stuck with a few more points if your opponent hits a prematurely early knock is relatively unimportant. Remember that the Gin bonus with extra boxes—either for you or the enemy—was at stake. This is partially true of Oklahoma Gin even when a higher knock-card is turned up. Points in your hand are not as important as they are in the standard game.

Suppose you get your three-card runs reasonably early, at a three- or two-point knock, and your tenth card is an Ace or a deuce. Do you go down or do you play for Gin? With an Ace up, that decision has been made for you. With a 2 or 3 up, that decision was made for you when you happened to acquire a four-card meld early in the play; in that case the coming-in of your third meld automatically gave you Gin.

With three three-carders and a low card, your decision on whether or not to go for the extra boxes is based on the answers to several questions. How early in the hand is it? How many cards in the deck can Gin you? Are some of them already in the discard pile or marked to be in your opponent's hand? What about your opponent? Has he taken up many cards? Or does he seem very dangerous for other reasons, such as the apparent wildness of his discards and the suspicious complete absence of several denominations of cards in the discard pile? (The very fact that we think our opponent is close to Gin often impels us to forego our Gin play and go down as a defensive measure to forestall him. At a low knock we should not fail to go down because we are afraid of being undercut, since this is most unlikely. If we continue to play for Gin, we do so not out of fear, but out of optimism.)

Another question to ask ourselves, in trying to decide on knocking or continuing the Gin effort, is: How does our immediately available discard look? (With three melds we obviously have only two choices.) And what's our prognostication concerning the danger in our very next discard? Finally, how does future discarding look in general, in case our Gin cards take their time in showing up?

The need to decide whether to knock or to play for Gin (with those lovely extra-box bonuses) arises very often, regardless of the size of the knock-card. When it's late in the hand, and we know our opponent must be down pretty low, the Gin bonuses loom even larger in proportion to the few points we expect to pick up. But let's see how we handle ourselves in a few specific situations. Assume we are "on" all three games, with therefore no danger of a skunk. (When such is not the case we rarely play for Gin.)

The diamond 2 was the up-card. After about our fifth draw, we happily find ourselves with these eleven cards:

Normally this is a hand on which the Gin bonuses would intrigue us. Five cards are available to Gin us; the heart 2 and the diamond Ace are fairly safe discards. But let's assume that certain other factors exist: We know our opponent has 10's (he took one and a sequence in that suit wasn't possible); so at least one, and probably both of the 10's to add to our runs will never appear. Also, *we* took up the heart 7 from the discard pile after another 7 had been discarded. So our opponent will never give us the heart 6 if he has it or gets it. If he has or gets it, he'll undoubtedly try to amass other 6's to go with it—thus about cutting in half our chances of getting the spade 6 also. Our apparently rosy Gin hopes have diminished to not too much more than the fourth 4. So we knock for one instead, settling for the box and whatever points come our way. (We might get a lot; it's fairly early in the hand.)

Say it's about halfway through the pack on this next hand, with a Jack as the up-card. We just drew our third Queen and have these eleven cards:

| Q♠ | Q♥ | Q♦ | J♦ | 9♥ | 9♦ | 9♣ | 7♠ | 6♠ | 5♣ | A♣ |

Since it's fairly late in the hand, and our opponent has at least one run that we know of, we can't expect too many points. The diamond Jack is a mighty safe discard. So we play on for Gin—with undercut probabilities also running for us if our opponent goes down with anything less than Gin.

But let's change the situation a bit. Our opponent has taken up two of our discards. Also, lots of combinations are extant, unbroken by the cards in the discard pile. And instead of the safe Jack to discard, our other unmatched card besides the Ace is a wild 8 (or a 3 or a 4). Discarding it—or the Ace—is too likely to Gin our opponent. In this altered situation we give up going for the Gin bonuses and knock for one as a combination offensive-defensive maneuver.

Here's another situation. The club 9 is the knock-card and about one-third of the way through the pack we arrive at this dilemma:

| K♠ | K♥ | K♦ | K♣ | Q♥ | J♥ | J♣ | 7♠ | 4♠ | 3♠ | 2♠ |

We could knock for seven and feel sure of winning some points. But let's say we have a good lead in points on all three games and now want some of those extra Gin boxes. Our opponent, furthermore, doesn't seem dangerous. So we decide to play for Gin. Having made that decision, we should go all out to bring about the desired end as quickly as possible.

The club Jack happens to be quite safe as a discard, the club 7 almost completely wild. But note that if we throw the Jack we have only three Gin cards. But keeping the Jack, even at the expense of probably helping the enemy by discarding the 7, should appear most attractive to us. Now either missing Jack will Gin us too (we then give up the heart run and meld four Kings and three Jacks), thus almost doubling our chances. So we should either knock for seven, or discard the seven and go for Gin in a thoroughgoing way.

Generally Gin Rummy—like most good card games—is a game of compromises and compromise plays. But in a situation like the above, and in many similar situations, you can't try to have your cake and eat it too. Take a position one way or the other.

13.

TAKING CARDS "ON SPEC"

Taking up cards "on spec" is a particularly appropriate matter for discussion when Oklahoma Gin is our over-all subject. For the benefit of those who are used to a different type of patois, "taking a card on spec" refers to picking up the original up-card, or any discard of our opponent, without said card giving us a new meld or even providing an addition to an existing meld in our hand.

The "spec," of course, stands for speculation. We take this card not because it gives us a meld, but because it gives us a new combination, the embryo of a new meld, which we firmly believe at the moment that we need in our business. Speculation or "spec" can sometimes be good business. But let's clarify immediately what constitutes a good or reasonable "spec" play as opposed to a downright foolish one.

If, for example, the club 9 is discarded and we take it up solely because we have another 9 in our hand—we have no nearby clubs —such a maneuver cannot be dignified by calling it a speculative play. Or if we take that club 9 just because we have the club 8 in our hand, that is an equally silly waste of time. We'll summarize the case by saying that, almost without exception, taking a discard on such slim provocation is bad Gin Rummy.

A legitimate "spec" play—provided everything else about the hand calls for preferring it to a pick from the stock—comes when the discard "hits" *two* cards in your hand. The discard is the same club 9 and you have in your hand another 9 and either the club 8 or the club 10. In taking up the club 9 you have created for yourself a combination which will develop into a meld with the assistance of any one of four cards (none of which we assume have appeared previously in the discard pile). A distinctly less advantageous, but possibly conceivable, "spec" play might consist of taking up the same club 9, holding another 9 and the club 7 or club Jack. This would create a combination for us which three cards could hit.

We hope we've given the impression to date that—and we firmly believe this—taking cards "on spec" is not a normal way of life for a winning Gin Rummy player. In the standard, 10-for-knock game, the hands that call for taking a card "on spec" are very few and far between. In Oklahoma Gin, with lower knock-cards going way down to the Ace (which insists that we Gin), we feel compelled to take "spec" cards somewhat more often. We are forced to play for three melds, if not precisely Gin. But how can you play for three melds if you have none or only one) in your hand and no good potential meld combinations?

Under such sad circumstances, drastic measures may be in order. We're hungry for melds and have learned that absolutely no hand we pick up at Gin should be deemed hopeless. Wonderful things can, and frequently do, happen if we are of stout heart and play intelligently. (At bridge, if we pick up a complete Yarborough and our partner passes originally, all we can hope for, barring a miracle, is a small loss.)

So, with quite a few hands—depending on their exact composition, the size of the up-card, and sometimes certain psychological or strategic reasons—we take a card "on spec." Meditate on the following hand.

Your opponent's initial discard is the spade 8. Both you and he had turned down the up-card. As first player, he had drawn from the stock. This is what you have:

I deliberately haven't identified the up- or knock-card because I want you to consider your possible action in such a situation with various possible knock-cards. Suffice it to say that the up-card could have been anything from an Ace to a picture card, and that it had no special or relevant relation to the cards in your hand. Let's first assume the up-card to have been the club Jack, permitting a knock for 10 or less.

The temptation to take up that spade 8 "on spec"—giving us a nice open-to-four-cards combination—does exist. But at a 10 knock it should be resisted for a number of reasons. First, what should we discard in its place? With the high knock we can't afford to give up any of our low cards. They're not only wild, but also give us a three-card "third meld," easily expandable into a four-carder. Also, if we discard any one of them our opponent, even though he doesn't take it for a real meld, may be able to use it for *his* "third meld" and obtain a quick knock thereby. As for splitting the Queens for discards, the absurdity of breaking one combination just to take up another is self-evident. Next, not taking up the spade 8 makes available to us two cards we can discard (our 9 and 8) with some degree of safety. To use a bridge analogy, taking the 8 will squeeze us; not taking it will do just the opposite. Finally, by drawing from the pack we do have some chance for a very quick knock; two fine draws (a Queen and any 4 or less) will do the trick.

At the same 10-knock, if we take the same hand and replace one of the Queens with the spade King we will have what looks like a hopeless horror to improve, with no combinations at all. In that case we would consider taking up the spade 8, since the four-way combination it gives us may be our only salvation. If we take it, we discard the King, of course. Actually, we feel sure that taking up the spade 8 on the changed hand is the correct play; we've used weasel words because, in general, we don't want to encourage "spec" plays at a 10-knock.

Going back to the original hand with the two Queens, let's assume the refused up-card was an Ace, 2 or 3. Now the "spec" play of taking up the spade 8 is correct for a variety of reasons. At the low-knock we have to go for three runs; the four-way combination the 8 gives us is a firm step in that direction. Furthermore, we are now much less squeezed—in fact, hardly at all. Whatever the low denomination of the up-card—remember that our opponent passed it up, too—it made all three of our low cards much safer as discards, insofar as giving our opponent a meld is concerned. Also, the lowness of the knock-card makes our low cards not dangerous merely because of their lowness.

To what extent should the spade 8 entice us with, say, a 6-point knock? We consider this a fairly close decision. We do have three small cards adding to 6, but we can't very well expect to improve this with a fourth low card. We're up to the maximum. So a four-card meld plus a three-carder will be needed. Thus the spade 8 tempts us. But if we take it up we'll have to throw a low card (and a dangerous one besides) and in effect be giving up a made three-card meld for a hoped-for-four-carder. Taking everything into consideration we should by-pass the 8, just as we would with a higher knock of from 7 to 10. We'll not be squeezed for a while anyway. We'll have the three low cards running for us as our second meld. And the two draws from the stock we'll be making, while throwing our 8 and 9, may bring new vitality to our hand.

14.

"SPADES DOUBLE"

We hinted earlier that when a spade turned up opens Oklahoma Gin our tactics shouldn't basically change, but our intestinal fortitude may need bolstering. If the Ace of spades happens to be the up-card, one of the players (barring the occasional hand that goes to the wall) is going to get five(!) boxes on each of three games, plus double a minimum of 25 points—and perhaps a lot more—also on three games. So if your opponent gives you a quick spade Gin, catching you with a lot in your hand—well, it only hurts for a second and you may as well be broke as the way you are.

But there is a point behind that flip philosophizing. You can't play scared just because a spade turns up. With a low knock-card throw a safe low card rather than a wild high card, spades or not. Play for the three runs you need. Go for Gin if your hand calls for it. Don't unload your high cards indiscriminately, breaking up your combinations solely to reduce expenses. In brief, don't panic. It's the same game of skill it was before a spade turned up, only the stakes are doubled.

Of course the fact that the point score is doubled does affect us in certain situations when the little black figures on the white score pad explicitly cry "Danger!" Let's say we're playing Hollywood and, though we've scored on the first two games, it's 80 to 0 against us on the third game. With that potential skunk staring us in the face, our woes are increased when the 10 of spades is turned up on the next deal. Nobody takes it. After we make our draw from the stock as first player, we are confronted with these unappetizing-looking eleven cards:

K♦ K♥ 9♠ 8♠ 7♦ 6♠ 4♣ 2♦ 2♣ 2♠ A♠ ▲

We have to discard, and here's how we should reason. We are in danger of being skunked on this hand if our opponent can engineer a fairly quick knock—which isn't too tough with 10 as the up-card. If he knocks for even the maximum of 10, and we have 45 points or more in our hand, we've had it. The 35 doubles to 70; 70 and 80 is 150!

This is a pretty bad hand and we don't really expect to win it. But normally we wouldn't give up on it; it's certainly possible to win it and get off the skunk right away. If it weren't a spade hand, we'd surely keep the Kings for a while—they're our only real offensive possibility—and risk throwing the heart 9 or perhaps the diamond 7. But the upturned spade has the skunk breathing down our necks. We must try to get our count down as quickly as possible to a point where a quick knock won't close us out. Then we'll have another chance to get on score on the next deal.

Let's see what splitting the Kings does for us. (The spade King goes first because of the refused upturned 10.) First they're surely our safest discards. (If the spade King is taken up, our second one will be a player.) If they are not taken we'll probably have a breathing spell for a while, unless our opponent is very lucky in drawing from the wall. After one King goes, our unmatched cards add up to 45 points. At our next draw, let's say we manage to pick a 3. The other King goes. We're now down to 37. Doubled, it's 74. But if our opponent now knocks for *anything more than two* we'll be below the 150 mark and the day will be saved for the nonce.

Another draw should get us to the point where only a Ginning by the enemy can schneider us. That we can't help. If we reach the safety point in unmatched cards and the hand is still alive, we can concentrate a bit on trying to win the hand, remote as it may seem. Our opponent may have a bad hand, too.

The above is one type of situation where the combination of spades and the state of the score forces us to play scared—but intelligently scared!

15.

"ADVERTISING"

Although the slang and patois of Gin Rummy varies greatly throughout the country (there are probably 10 other expressions for what we in these articles have called schneider *and* blitz *and* skunk) we think the term "advertising" will be recognized as meaning the same thing in any game anywhere.

So it is almost superfluous for me to explain that "advertising" means discarding a card in the hope that this "ad" will extract, as an early discard from your opponent, some relative or mate of your discard.

You throw an odd King or 10 at your first opportunity because you have a matched Queen-Jack in another suit crying for company. (Three's never a crowd at Gin Rummy.) Or you discard, say, the spade 8 because you have the club and diamond 9's in your hand, hoping that the discard will extract the spade 9 from his hand if he has it. Or, ideally, you may have a double or triple advertiser. You throw the spade 6. The spade 5 will give you fives; the heart 6 and club 6 will give you runs in those suits. And so on. The perfect situation is to make a discard which has both relative safety and advertising value.

There is no doubt that it pays to advertise. But, paradoxical as it may seem, it *does not pay* to try to "guess" your opponent's advertisers and very proudly *not* fall for them. A good Gin player is never crestfallen if he follows his opponent's discards with matching or touching cards from his own hand and finds that they are taken up occasionally. If your opponent throws the spade 8 as his first discard, are you supposed to hold up a loose 8 and a loose spade 9 in your hand? The answer is NO, no matter how suspicious you are. Are you going to keep your hand cluttered up with non-working cards and make even more dangerous discards instead, just because you hate hucksters?

Your opponent's first discard is a 6, his second a Queen. You acquire a 6 in your hand at your second draw. If you're of the school that believes it also pays to resist the advertiser, you'll say something like this to yourself: "Oh ho, so he throws a low card like a 6 before a high, safer Queen. Does he think he's playing with children? He'll not get that 6 out of me till I'm ready to go down." So out goes a wild card instead. Furthermore, with only 9 cards to work with, our hero probably will never get down. And all the while the opponent who threw the 6 before the Queen likely as not did so solely because it was a safer card from his view; he may have had another 6 in a run or the matching 7 as part of three 7's—or even both. If he was advertising with the 6, the odds are still against the fact that the particular related card you have available to discard (in this case another 6) is the specific card he was advertising for.

So it is not a contradiction to say that you should advertise as much as you can, within reasonable limits of safe discarding, and that you should not be overly wary of your opponent's doing the same thing. It costs no more to give an opponent a meld when you respond to a suspected advertiser, than it does to give him a meld by throwing a completely wild card. The latter maneuver is more likely to give him a meld.

Of course, you should play your individual opponents a bit. If you know the fellow across the table from you to be the naive type who *always* throws an advertiser on his very first play, or one who *never* throws an early low card unless it is an advertiser, respond to this knowledge in solving a *borderline* choice-of-discard situation. But don't overdo it.

16.

ADVANCED PSYCHOLOGICAL PLAYS

There's a tremendous variety to Gin Rummy—and to the Oklahoma version in particular—which is not apparent to inexperienced players. Many fine plays—deviating greatly from the norm, but sound from a psychological and strategic angle—are yours for the making, if you can see them. Here are a couple of top-level examples:

The spade 2 is the knock-card. It's about halfway through the pack. We know our opponent is going all out for Gin—because he's that type, because 2 is the knock-card and he's been throwing Aces, and finally because he's already taken two cards. (We know he has 9's and Queens, probably four of one of them.) He likely has some four-way combination in the 4 and 5 area, since none of those cards has appeared although three 6's have been discarded. He now discards the club 2 and here is our holding at this point:

It's our plan to stop his going Gin. Although we like Gin bonuses ourselves, we'd be very happy in this dangerous situation to stop him by going down as quickly as possible without Ginning. Remember that the spade 2 was dealt and passed up by both players. Let's see what taking up that club 2 might do for us. Obviously it gives us a 2 to go down with if we get a third meld. We feel sure we don't have time to get both a third meld and, in addition, one of only three possible players on our melds to go Gin. Most important: If we take up the club 2, our opponent doesn't know we are taking it just as a potential knock card. Since the club 3 is in our hand, not his, he most probably will

think we took the 2 for a club run. Thus, with the club 3 used by
us in a run, other 3's will seem relatively safe to him as discards.

So we take up the club 2 and split our 10's. They are 100 per
cent safe from runs, and the possibility that he is holding specifically the other two 10's as his Gin hope is most remote. He drew
from the stock and—yes, this was an actual hand we played—as
we had hoped, out came the spade 3. We took it and knocked for
2. He had three Queens, four 9's, the spade and heart 5's and the
heart 4 left in his hand. The spade 3 had been his logical discard,
but we won 12 doubled, or 24 points. P.S.: The next two cards in
the stock were the heart 6 and a 5.

Here's another off-beat strategem. (Don't make these plays
unless you've been around a bit; you may badly misread things.)
It's about the middle of a hand with an Ace up, making Gin the
forced knock. You hold:

| Q♥ | 10♥ | 10♦ | 10♣ | 6♥ | 5♥ | 5♦ | 2♠ | 2♥ | 2♣ | ♣ |

You've just split Queens on the previous play and the heart
Queen is now 100 per cent safe. Your opponent draws from the
stock and throws the 6 of clubs.

Pick it up as a sound psychological maneuver and unload the
Queen. The 6 adds to your chances for a third run. You can
always throw it back later if you improve elsewhere, or if you
badly need a safe discard in the end game. In the meantime it
may, among other things, squeeze your opponent by forcing him
to hold on to another 6 or some adjacent club. What's more, it
does a great deal towards confusing your opponent as to what
you actually do have. This will greatly improve the chances of his
giving you the spade 5, the heart 7 or the heart 4.

Of course a play like this, in a situation where circumstances
are just right, doesn't mean that we should forget cardinal princi-
ples. We had that 100-per-cent-safe discard, and taking up the
club 6 was done mainly to throw a red herring across the trail. It
was a form of what we might call "misadvertising." The fact that
the play also gave us a new combination was almost (not quite)
an incidental extra advantage. We're by no means trying to
negate the general rule that it doesn't pay to pick up a purely
"spec" card in the middle game and with a good hand.

17.

SOME RULES AND CUSTOMS

When playing Hollywood, three games at a time, most groups like to score the last game at double. This is a logical equalizing move. For most of the game your scores go on the pad three times. But, too often, two games get completed fairly soon and the third game may go on for quite a few hands. So, to keep the interest up to normal, the third-game final total is doubled.

In most circles a hand is not played all the way through the stock. The hand is considered over after a discard is made with only two cards remaining in the stock. This is a sensible regulation. It gives a player fighting a valiant defensive battle a better chance of "forcing the hand to the wall," which means getting a tie—no score—on the hand. (More on forcing a hand to the wall in the next chapter.)

If you played the hand down to the very end of the stock, the last player would now have a mathematical certainty. He'd know for sure exactly what his opponent holds (and the next-to-last player would know it within one card.) This knowledge would be available by carefully going through the entire discard pile, if that is permitted, or through perfect memorization. Either way it would be time-consuming and the final decision would be completely unspeculative and require no judgment. All of which is contrary to the spirit of the game.

Gin Rummy is not a game requiring complicated rules and penalities. The lawyers are rarely needed. But suppose a player takes two cards from the stock accidentally, as so often happens, or takes up only one but sees the next one in the process. Something must be done to compensate the opponent. The most popular, and best, solution to this one is as follows: The offender keeps his correct card and the other one is put face up alongside the discard pile. The offender discards and now his opponent has the choice of taking that extra exposed card, or taking the offender's discard, or drawing from the stock. If he doesn't take the exposed card, the offender in turn has the same choices, but the first option was the more important one. If neither takes the exposed card, it is now a dead discard. This sensible rule is made to cancel out, rather than punish, the inadvertent offense.

We believe all other irregularities should be treated in this spirit. Some of the rules in the books, played by some groups, should be dispensed with in friendly games. For example, if a player says "I knock for 10" and then notices, before anything else has been done, that it's a three knock and corrects himself, no harm has been done. We believe that, in all fairness, the hand can continue with no penalty. Some people believe he should be forced to show his hand to prove he was actually down to 10. If you can't believe in your opponent's honesty, we feel that you shouldn't play with him. Furthermore, he's paid you a bit for his inadvertence by letting you know he's down as low as 10.

Similarly, if a player puts down his hand, announcing Gin, and then you both notice he isn't Gin, there's no need to be too rough on him. If he is low enough to go down with Ginning (depending on the up-card) he is simply considered to have knocked for the total of his unmatched cards. If he can't knock under the conditions of the deal, he simply picks up his cards and play resumes. He's paid enough of a penalty by having allowed you to see his entire hand. Fie on those who would want him to play out the hand completely exposed, with each new draw seen by the opponent.

You should of course protect yourself, when your opponent knocks, by inspecting his hand to see that everything is in order, before showing yours and before making any announcements as to what you're stuck with. And you should expect your opponent to do the same.

18.

SOME TRICKS OF
THE TRADE

The astute player frequently throws a card which he *knows* will play on a meld held by his opponent, rather than throw a new wild card. This is done because it is his best judgment that, at this particular stage of this particular hand, giving the enemy a new meld will be fatal, whereas a single-card addition to a meld will not help as much.

Sometimes such a play is a virtual certainty. Say an Ace is turned up and we must play for Gin. Early in the hand our opponent took up a 9; a bit later we gave him another 9—we had to guess between that card and a touching 8 and guessed wrong. We also know he has three Queens. At certain point we draw the fourth Queen from the wall and must select a discard. Our other choices may give him his third run; obviously we don't have much to choose from, since we are trying to Gin ourselves. We unhesitatingly throw the Queen. Since presumably he already has his one four-card meld, a second four-carder will not normally help him towards Ginning. But any other discard not 100 per cent safe can get the job done—for him, not us.

Here's a type of play which should be in your repertoire. With the 10 of clubs as the knock-card, here are your eleven cards after your first draw:

You are in a wonderful position for a quick killing. Any 4-spot or lower will put you down and also either of two 6's or two 10's, with the latter "advertised for" by the up-card. You're odds on to make it within the next few picks. Either the heart Queen or club 5 must go now, with the former being a shade safer. But you should throw the 5. If that gives him a meld he will reduce expenses—for the quick knock you have in store for him—only by about 15 points. But if the Queen hits him he'll save about 30 points. The 5 additional points you could get out of your own hand is literally of no consequence; he's not very likely to go down at this stage.

Incidentally, there's one more argument in favor of the 5 of clubs discard against an experienced opponent. It is likely to get the diamond or spade 6 (or a 4) out of him very promptly, since presumably he is aware of the safe discarding theory expounded in an earlier article. (An early discard doesn't come from a combination; hence you don't have the club 6; hence a 6 has only one chance of giving you 6's.)

The "free play" theory in Gin Rummy is about as fallacious as the so-called "free double" in bridge. Suppose you deal, your opponent refuses the up-card and you take it up because it connects with *one* card in your hand, or because it's fairly low—a 3 or 4—and you want to unload a useless high card. You do so, knowing you're not helping your cause very much, on the theory that you're getting this turn on the house since your opponent gets the first draw from the stock anyway. Briefly, you think it "costs you nothing." But that's the point—it may cost you a great deal in exchange. You're the one who's now going to have to make the first discard, and open up those dangerous new vistas. We'd prefer to have the enemy give us the first discarding clue on a hand, rather than give it to him.

Naturally the "free play" theory is not completely invalid. If the price is right you may sometimes accept a "free" ride. Suppose the up-card, refused by your opponent, is the heart 4. You're playing the standard knock-for-10 game. Here is your hand:

| K♥ | J♥ | 10♥ | 9♥ | 8♠ | 7♦ | 6♠ | 4♣ | 2♥ | A♥ |

The heart 4 gives you a pair of 4's and also ties in with the heart 2 and you badly need a new combination somewhere. The heart King is available as a discard that has some degree of safety. And you're not sacrificing a draw from the stock to take up that heart 4. All these little advantages together add to a sufficient reason for you to be willing to accept the disadvantage of making the first discard.

19.

FORCING A DRAW

The ultimate in defensive play is "forcing a hand to the wall." Once the final discard is made and not taken up, with only two cards remaining in the stock, the hand is over and there is no decision. When you have a bad hand and can't get down low enough to knock safely (or go Gin if that is required) the next best thing is to do your best to keep your opponent in the same fix.

Forcing a hand to the wall is never your immediate objective at the start of a hand. Even the most hopeless-seeming hands can improve tremendously after a few draws, so don't indulge in extreme pessimism. Even if you take a dim view of your chances to win the hand, you have to start off by trying. The campaign ahead of you is too long and too uncontrollable to make worthwhile any immediate effort towards forcing a draw.

But you do play your bad hands conservatively and make every effort to discard as safely as possible. You keep hanging on and, somewhere along about the middle of the hand, you find you're still alive and that a silver lining shows signs of appearing behind the clouds. Not that your own hand has become a thing of beauty —your chances of going down and winning still seem dismal. But more and more avenues to possible melds are becoming closed to your opponent. He too may never be able to get down. Even if he can, he may be afraid to—now that it's later in the hand. (You, we presume, haven't shown any *outward* signs of distress. The junk you hold may be three melds as far as he's concerned.)

Obviously, the best chance of forcing a hand to the wall occurs when an Ace is turned up and your opponent (as well as you) must go Gin. In general, the lower the up-card the better are your chances. With a 2 or 3 as the knock-card it takes almost as long to get down as to Gin; likely as not your opponent has committed himself to Gin or nothing.

Here is an example of the extreme to which you can go in defending. You're playing Oklahoma, so the spade Ace which was turned up means Gin or no count. Here's your hand after drawing from a stock which has only about eight pickable cards now left in it:

You know your opponent has Queens and 7's. You've carefully noticed the discards and you know that all other high melds from 6's up are no longer available, sequences included. All the Aces are gone, so your friend across the table will have to do big things in the 2, 3 or 4 department if he is to Gin you. Furthermore, his *four-card* meld will have to be in that direction, since you have his fourth Queen and his fourth 7. Unless your inventory has been inaccurate, you now should know that your opponent cannot possibly go Gin provided you don't let him at your 2, 3, 4, 7 or Queen. Those odd rocks are as valuable as jewels to you, as long as they remain in your hand.

The only way you can keep all of those cards is by breaking up your Jacks (or your 5's, if you're careful of the spade department which could give a four-card sequence there.) But this shouldn't be hard for you to do. Your own chances for Ginning are just about nil. It may be displeasing to your eyes or your sense of symmetry to see two odd Jacks in your hand where previously there had been three. But the artist in you, not only the Gin Rummy artist, should be very proud once one of those Jacks hits the table.

You'll now be sure of carrying the hand down to the last two cards. Future discards will automatically take care of themselves. Forgetting the other Jacks, which are available, all other cards you draw will either be 100 per cent safe, or at least "Ginproof," as a discard. Even a second 4, 3 or 2, which you may draw and discard after your Jacks are gone, cannot Gin him as long as you keep its mate.

One word of warning. Don't make a play of this type with some higher knock-card unless you're absolutely sure of your ground. We once saw a fellow proudly break three Jacks at his last discard, with only the two unplayable cards left in the stock, forgetting the up-card had been a 10. His opponent was aware of what was going on and had three three-card melds and the fourth Jack in his hand. He promptly picked up the discarded Jack and knocked for ten with it, discarding his own Jack. Our muddled friend was stuck with two Jacks, plus a couple of other unmelded cards which he had seen fit to retain in the interest of safety.

20.

PARTNERSHIP GIN

Partnership gin, for four (or six or eight) players, still retains its basic identity as a two-handed man-to-man game. I play against you; at the same time my partner plays against your partner with a different deck. But both hands must be completed before going on to another deal, since the results of the two hands are combined to make one team entry on the score card.

The game is almost always played Hollywood (three games at a time) style. Though it can be played either the standard 10-to-knock or the Oklahoma way, we'll assume it's the latter for purposes of this discussion. The variations (extra boxes, etc.) of Oklahoma which add to the fun and excitement and skill of two-handed play, do so even more when you play partnership Gin.

If you get me for 23 points on a deal, but my partner Gins your partner and picks up 10 points besides for a total of 35 (25 Gin bonus, plus 10), my side wins a net of 12 points. We get the 12 points on one, two or three games—depending on how many games we were on previously—just as in regular Hollywood. We get the automatic box which goes with the entered score and (since it's Oklahoma) we get two extra boxes for my partner's Ginning.

If both partners win, their scores are added to each other and the total is entered. If both partners go Gin, they get four extra boxes, two for each Gin. (And eight if it's spades.) If there's a Gin for one player on each side in any hand, some partnership fans say the Gins cancel each other out and give no extra boxes; others give the two boxes to the side which has won the hand on the point differential.

At partnership Oklahoma Gin it is best, for a variety of reasons, for both hands to be played for the same knocking point—even though the two dealt up-cards are different, as they usually are.

The usual rule is that the lower of the two up-cards is automatically taken as the knocking point for *both* contests. If you and I turned up an Ace on the deal and our partners turned up a 10—and the rule was that we'd have to go for Gin and they could knock for 10—the chances are they'd have to wait around quite a while after they finished their hand for us to finish ours.

The game-ending point at four-handed should be jacked up to 200. With scores being added together, and spade hands, and frequent Ginning, the skunks would come too fast and furiously for most people's pleasure at a 150-point game objective. They come pretty often even at 200.

There are two cardinal points to remember in playing partnership Gin, Hollywood style. One, winning the box is *the thing*. Get on the three scores at all cost. You save getting skunked that way and simultaneously keep the opponents "on the skunk." Two, you must frequently sacrifice your own hand's maximum possibilities to achieve that goal of winning the box. Points One and Two obviously are interrelated.

Briefly, here's what you try to do: If partner goes down while you're still playing, and gives you a "cushion," do your darndest to protect it. If, for example, he won 38 points (with or without a Gin bonus included) you know your opponent is going to have to try to go Gin to get it back. So, if you can, you must try to get your own unmelded cards down to 12 points or less so that, even if your opponent Gins, you still retain one point of the cushion and win the box. You do this even at the expense of minimizing your own chances of winning a bundle of points or Ginning on your own.

Once you've reached the magic number in unmatched cards (12, in this case) you can, box secured, go all out for Gin on your own hook. If you get it, your combined team score will be very easy to take.

Similarly, if your partner's opponent goes down early, leaving you with a sizeable deficit, it is up to you, within reason, to try to make it up. You try to Gin on hands which normally mightn't call for such action. But remember that "within reason." *Keep close tabs on the back score.* Often it's best merely to try to reduce expenses a bit and hope for better luck on the next hand. If you press, you might lose a skunk or two on the single deal.